WILDLIFE IN BLOOM SERIES

Little Snake

BY AUTHOR & CONSERVATIONIST

LINDA BLACKMOOR

ISBN: 978-1-966417-26-2 (PRINT)

PUBLISHED BY QUILL PRESS. LINDA BLACKMOOR'S TITLES MAY BE
PURCHASED IN BULK FOR EDUCATIONAL, BUSINESS, FUNDRAISING, OR
SALES PROMOTIONAL USE. FOR INFORMATION, PLEASE EMAIL
HELLO@LINDABLACKMOOR.COM

FIRST PRINT EDITION: 2025

LINDA BLACKMOOR
WWW.LINDABLACKMOOR.COM

SPECIES

Snakes are reptiles in the suborder Serpentes, with over 3,000 species found on every continent except Antarctica. Their sizes range from tiny threadsnakes measuring only 4 inches (10 cm) to giant anacondas exceeding 30 feet (9 m). They evolved from lizard-like ancestors, losing their limbs over millions of years. Today, snakes inhabit deserts, forests, wetlands, oceans, and even mountains.

SNAKE FACTS #2

ANATOMY

A snake's body is elongated and limbless, equipped with flexible backbones made up of hundreds of vertebrae. Their skulls have specialized joints that allow them to open their jaws extremely wide to swallow large prey. Many species have reduced or no left lung, making room for other organs in their narrow bodies. This streamlined shape enables snakes to slither into tight spaces and move with stealth.

SNAKE FACTS #3

SKIN

Snakes have scaly skin made of keratin, the same material in human hair and nails. These scales overlap and protect snakes from abrasions, while also aiding in movement across various surfaces. Between the scales are tiny skin folds that stretch when they eat large meals. By periodically shedding, or molting, snakes replace old skin cells and remove parasites.

SENSES

Snakes rely on chemoreception, using their forked tongues to collect scent particles and transfer them to the Jacobson's organ. This organ helps them track prey, find mates, and recognize their surroundings even with poor eyesight. Some species, like pit vipers, have heat-sensing pits to detect warm-blooded animals in the dark. Their hearing is limited to sensing vibrations through the ground.

SNAKE FACTS #5

MOVEMENT

Most snakes slither by pushing against the ground with their muscles and scales, creating wave-like motions. Some move in straight lines by inching their belly scales forward, while others can "sidewind" across loose sand. Tree-dwelling snakes coil around branches, stretching from one branch to another with agility. Their diverse locomotion styles allow them to live in habitats ranging from deserts to treetops.

SNAKE FACTS #6

DIET

Snakes are carnivores, primarily feeding on rodents, birds, frogs, eggs, or other reptiles, depending on the species. They swallow prey whole, thanks to flexible jaws that expand to fit large meals. Some constrictors like boas and pythons coil around prey to suffocate it before swallowing. By controlling rodent populations, many snake species also help maintain ecological balance.

VENOM

Around 600 snake species are venomous, producing toxins in glands behind the eyes, delivered via hollow or grooved fangs. Venoms kill or immobilize prey, and can also protect snakes from predators. Different venom types affect prey in various ways: damage to blood cells by hemotoxins or neurotoxins attacking the nervous system. Snake venom research helps develop medicines for heart conditions and more.

BABIES

Snakes reproduce through oviparity (egg-laying) or viviparity (live birth), depending on the species. Some species, like garter snakes, give birth to fully formed young, whereas pythons lay clutches of eggs they may coil around for protection. Incubation temperatures can influence the development speed and even the sex of some hatchlings. Parental care is rare.

MOLTING

Snakes shed their skin in a process called ecdysis, which can happen several times a year. Their eyes appear milky or bluish before shedding because a fluid separates the old skin from the new layer underneath. This process helps them get rid of parasites and allows growth. Shedding often occurs in one piece, leaving behind a delicate, see-through skin that mirrors the snake's scale pattern.

SNAKE FACTS #10

DEFENSE

Many snakes have unique defense tactics, from camouflage and warning coloration to bluffing strikes and hissing displays. Some, like the hognose snake, play dead by rolling onto their backs with open mouths and limp bodies. Venomous species may display bright colors or rattling tails to warn predators away. Nonvenomous ones often rely on speed, cryptic coloration, or mimicry of venomous snakes for protection.

HISS

Though snakes are often silent, some use hisses or rubbing scales together to produce warning sounds. The rattlesnake's infamous tail shake is a clear example of communication, signaling threats to back off. Scent trails left by females help males track potential mates. Head or body movements can also convey defensive messages or readiness to strike.

SNAKE FACTS #12

LONGEVITY

In the wild, snake lifespans range from a few years up to two decades, depending on species and environmental factors. Boas, pythons, and some vipers can live over 20 years in the wild or captivity. Smaller snakes typically have shorter lives, influenced by predation and habitat challenges. Captive snakes with proper care often exceed wild lifespans due to consistent food and shelter

SNAKE FACTS #13

BRUMATION

In cold climates, many snakes enter brumation, a state similar to hibernation, when temperatures drop. They seek sheltered dens or burrows—sometimes sharing with other snake species—to conserve energy through the winter. During brumation, snakes eat very little and rely on stored body fat for survival, becoming sluggish until warmth returns. As spring arrives, they emerge to bask in the sun.

www.ingramcontent.com/pod-product-compliance
Lightning Source LLC
Chambersburg PA
CBHW060838270326
41933CB00002B/123

9 7 8 1 9 6 6 4 1 7 2 6 2